Massive Purpose.

MW01169287

The Athlete's Success Planner

Created and Designed by: Coach Jason P. Beeding

www.jasonbeeding.com

First Edition 2019
ISBN: 978-0-359-93158-3

Distributed in Part By: ARM - All Reps Matter

Massive Purpose.   Relentless Intent.   Super Success.

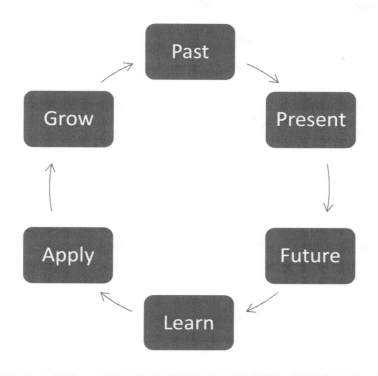

The Athlete's Success Planner

This planner is designed to guide you on a journey to athletic success. Success comes when athletes, who are determined to be their very best, become obsessed with the process behind their training, mental state and game play. Their absolute motivation to become their very best overcomes any level of self-doubt they might have. The effective execution of their goals provides a guiding light to success

What describes or defines an athlete? A simple description is that athletes train in movement. Some defining features are strength, stamina, mobility and agility. However, an often-overlooked measurement is their mental and emotional state. Yes, being explosive, strong and balanced matters but what is the plan for getting bigger, faster & stronger? How do you handle your emotions as they present themselves? This planner's strategy is to help you figure that out by using MRS:

Massive purpose. Relentless Intent. Super Success.

The Athlete's Success Planner was developed as a result of not being content with the availability of products in the market that are athlete-goal specific. The Athlete's Success Planner presents a method for athletes to track and to weigh their progress. My focus is on healthy habit-building to help athletes become more aware of their training and performance behaviors. This planner integrates best practices of planning and development into a unique method to construct a foundation to achieve peak mental state for training. By taking the flow energy within you and combining that with complete mental focus and immersion into your training and competition enhances your abilities to learn and grow putting you into a peak state.

This success planner is simple to use and is designed for you to actually want to use it as a tool to track your goals, improvements, and positive habit building. Remember, you can achieve anything you set your mind to as long as you have massive purpose, action, relentless intent, and determination behind the goals you set for yourself. I am honored to help you on this journey for athletic success.

The Daily *GAP* Challenge

I'd like to present to you a specific way to think about your day using an easy to remember acronym *GAP*. This stands for Goals, Actions and Planning. One of my challenges to you is for you to create and write down a daily *GAP* for yourself to operate from. You will want each day's *GAP* to start with a specific goal or set of goals. These are goals to help you reach a smaller takeaway from each day which will allow you to build up your massive purpose, relentless intent, thus reaching your ultimate athletic life goal and super success you are creating for yourself.

Once you have your smaller daily goal or goals set, you will look at what actions can you take in that day to achieve the goal or goals that you set. These actions will be specific to reaching your goals just for that day. Why? Because if you try to swallow the elephant in one bite, it is simply impossible and you will be overwhelmed. However, if you take small bites you can do it and you are more mentally capable of processing the task as achievable.

Let's look at an example.

Today I'm setting a small goal of heading to the gym at 6:00 am and I want to specifically concentrate on just my shoulder strength. I now have my goal, right? That goal for the day is to work on my shoulder strength. But notice one thing I did here. I added a time stamp to it. By adding in a time stamp it gives me some clarity to when and it helps my *GAP* building as I head into my planning for that day. Now let's test the action. The action I take is to do what? Do whatever it takes, within reason, to get to the gym at 6:00 am. This can be walking, driving my car, taking the bus or even using a donkey if that makes sense for you. What matters is that you try to do whatever it takes. Now that you have the goal and you have the action you can take to achieve that goal, you effectively have a plan. It's as simple as that.

Each day fill out the relevant "Control Your Day [S.M.A.R.T] worksheet with GAP in mind. The S.M.A.R.T. acronym is to help you further enhance the focus level of your goal / goals. Chop up your day by asking yourself these questions. Is my goal specific? Is my goal measurable? Is the goal achievable for that day? Is the goal relevant? Is the goal time bound?

Specific

In order to keep focused on your efforts, make your goal as clear and specific as possible. This will help you maintain motivation as you work towards it.

Measurable

It's critical to have quantifiable objectives, so you can keep tabs on your development and remain propelled. Surveying progress encourages you to remain engaged, fulfill your time constraints, and feel the energy of drawing nearer to accomplishing your objective.

Achievable

Your objective likewise should be sensible and feasible to be effective. At the end of the day, it should extend your capacities yet stay conceivable. When you set a feasible objective, you might have the option to recognize recently neglected chances or assets that can carry you closer to it.

Relevant

This progression is tied in with guaranteeing that your objective issues to you, and that it likewise lines up with other important objectives. We as a whole need backing and help with accomplishing our objectives, yet it's imperative to hold command over them.

Time Bound

Each objective needs a deadline, with the goal that you have a due date to concentrate on and something to progress in the direction of. This piece of the SMART objective criteria keeps regular assignments from taking need over your more extended term objectives.

Plan Your Athlete's Life of Success

What do you want out of life as an athlete?

Set your athletic goal as high as you want. Know what you want and get focused towards that goal. Expand your mind and dream big. Shoot for the moon on your ultimate goal.

How will you know when you have reached your athletic outcome?

Know what you want out of your life as an athlete in terms of your goal, create a measurable set of outcomes and know what measurements you will use to help you accomplish those goals.

When do you want to reach your athletic life goal?

Set a specific date. Your mind will work towards your goal better if you have a deadline.

Why do you want to accomplish this goal as an athlete?

The reasons you want to accomplish your athletic goal need to be understood. The reason you want to achieve this goal needs to be huge in order for you to keep the fire burning. Dissatisfaction with your current state leads to motivation and your motivation will help you see your goal achieved.

What roadblocks are standing in your way of your ultimate goal?

Describe the obstacles that are prohibiting you from accomplishing your ultimate goal. As you understand these obstacles more you will be able to overcome them faster.

What do you need to let go of?

List poor habits that are limiting your actions towards success as an athlete.

What new habits, values and traits do you need to acquire to reach your goal?

In order to effectively change as an athlete, you must change your beliefs.

Plan Your Athlete's Year of Success

What is your one-year goal as an athlete?

As you have now laid out your ultimate goal as an athlete, let's look at your goal as you see it coming about this year. What goals can we achieve this year to get you closer to your ultimate outcome?

_____
_____
_____
_____

What is your 6-month athlete goal?

Break down your one-year goal to something more controllable. What can you accomplish in the next 6 months to reach your one-year goal?

_____
_____
_____
_____

What is your 12-week athletic goal?

Now that you have your 6-month athlete goal set, let's break it down a little further. In order to get to your ultimate athlete life goal, it helps to break it down into bite size pieces that are more manageable.

_____
_____
_____
_____

"Don't limit your future based on your past, you won't get very far." - Jim Rohn

What is standing in your way?

List obstacles getting in your way. Let's really define these issues so you can achieve what you want.

_____
_____
_____
_____

What bad habits do you need to lose?

Open your mind to your habits that are limiting your ultimate success. Shed them by writing them down and letting them go.

_____
_____
_____
_____

List of Four Role models. Who can you grow and learn from?

Surround yourself with information from athletes, trainers, coaches, etc. that you look up to. Find successful people you can count on to bring you insight on your journey as an athlete.

_____
_____
_____
_____

Super Success Support Group

The purpose behind your super success support group is to assist you with a list of close-nit relationships that will help you stay focused and motivated on your quest to achieve your ultimate goal.   One of your greatest resources in life is the people you know and build report with. The more people you know the more resources you will have available to you as you strive to reach and accomplish your goals.   Look around often and strive to invite new people into your life.

You will want to find available coaches, trainers, athletes, teachers, anyone you can count on with some level of knowledge greater than yours as it relates to moving you forward.   These key individuals will help you discover the answers to your questions on a personal level.   Assemble a team of **10** key people with whom you have shared your ultimate goal and call upon them when the time is right to make counter moves against any self-doubt that might show up.   Don't worry if you don't have 10 right away. Just list as many as you can at this moment.   As you progress on your journey you can grow and make changes that make sense for your list.

Name	Phone #	Email

Now that you have your advisory team assembled, forge ahead with confidence in accomplishing your ultimate goal.   Rest assured that the people you have selected will have your back and help you succeed. Remember these people will help define who you will become and will help you get there, so take care of them as a valued, priceless treasure.

Are You Fully Committed?

The defining moment in reaching your ultimate athlete goal, all starts with you living up to whatever it takes to completing it. Are you 100% willing to give up bad habits, negative thoughts and poor work routines? Are you willing to learn more and train harder than you ever have in your life? Your preparedness and burning desire to be the athlete you need to be is what will set your plan into action. The belief and acknowledgement that you can and will be someone and something different than your current self that will help drive you forward to mental and physical betterment. Knowing what you want out of being an athlete is setting the plan. Your actions are what will lead you to fulfilling your plan, leading you to your success as an athlete. You must have massive purpose, relentless intent and take action in order to change. This is crucial to moving forward. Having purpose in your actions is the motivational fuel to accomplish what you want.

> "A real decision is measured by the fact that you've taken a new action. If there's no action, you haven't truly decided." – Tony Robbins

List below actions you can take RIGHT NOW to set you on your path. Don't skip this section, you must do it. Commit yourself to whatever it's going to take to get you where you want to be as an athlete.

Actions I Can Take RIGHT NOW!

1. _____
2. _____
3. _____
4. _____
5. _____

Putting your signature to this page means you now fully and whole heartedly commit to take ownership of your new committed self. You commit to the purpose, intent and actions it is going to take to get you to your ultimate athlete goal.

Signed: _____ Date Committed: _____

Taking Control of Your Week

The Morning Routine

Motivated, successful athletes don't just lay around in the morning. They have a dedicated morning routine that includes exercise, reading, meditation and visualization. Beyond the GAP challenge for each day athletes ARM themselves with their morning preparation. If you truly want athletic success you have to do the things that will set you apart from the rest.

Here is a 30-minute morning routine we put together modeled after those of some successful athletes. This is a great place to start to live out your plan of action. You can modify this as needed to best fit your time and life style. The important thing is that you start.

- Visualize your day and goal: 5 min
- Meditate on what you want to accomplish today: 5 min
- Hydration: Drink 12 ounces of water right after meditation
- Dynamic stretching: 10 min
- Read something positive in the morning like a motivational quote to jump-start positive daily thoughts: 2 min
- Write down things that you will do today that will help you reach your weekly goals: 3 min
- Contrast Shower: 5 min

Weekly Goals

At the beginning of each week fill out your weekly goal-setting sheet defining what you want to accomplish in the week that will get you closer to your ultimate goal.

Training Days

Write one or two words that you will commit to for that specific day towards reaching your weekly goals. For example, Monday you write "strength training". Setting the entire week upfront will put your training goals into action as if you have already accomplished them.

Taking Control of Your Week

Weekly Drills

Weekly drills will be any athletic drill that you will commit to for the day just the same as you did for your training. Write in a short blurb word that has meaning to you for that drill. An example of this would be: Balance. You have now committed to working on your balancing drills as an athlete for that week. This will work hand in hand with your daily GAP process.

Power "C's" to Reflect On

This is one of the most valuable portions of The Athlete's Success Planner. I have developed powerful and meaningful definitions of "C" words as they relate to athletes. These will be some extremely valuable words to live by as an athlete so take note and convert them to fuel to power your day, week, month and ultimately, life. Having these key word definitions in your back pocket will promote a healthy approach to helping you accomplish your athlete goals. Become a mental and emotional giant in your sport.

You will take **1** to 7 "C" words I've listed and work on them throughout your week's goals. The idea behind these words is to help you expand your level of awareness towards becoming the athlete you want to be. Try to reflect and utilize your inner thoughts behind each words significance as it relates to your life and whom your want to become.

> **"Since everything is a reflection of our minds, everything can be changed by our minds."**
> **- Buddha**

Taking Control of Your Week

Control

As an athlete you want to first master control over your mental state. In order to accomplish positive change in your athletic career, focus on things you want to accomplish rather than things you don't want or don't want to happen. Try to be in a "now state of mind". Ask yourself what I can do now in this moment to get closer to my goals. Perhaps it's listening to a motivational speech in the car or watching or studying a role model's mechanical preparation. Control your focus on opportunities vs. obstacles. Control what you can control and only focus on things within your control. For example, you can't control the umpire's call but you can control your delivery of the ball. Here is a short list of some things you can control: Actions, Emotions, Mental preparation, Visualization, Health, Training, Performance and All other Power "C" words to come. The most important take away from this Power "C" is controlling your habits and controlling your level of focus. Strive to create positive habits to help you accomplish your ultimate athlete goal.

Commitment

Controlling your level of commitment is going to be extremely important. Success as an athlete starts with the commitment to yourself to be better in every aspect in every way. If you fail to live up to your commitment as an athlete you will never fully realize your definitive goal as an athlete. Some things you can commit to as an athlete. Your training, purpose, intent, actions, beliefs, game play, etc. Athletes need to commit to the belief that they can and will be better athletes in order to reach their full potential.

> "Control your own destiny or someone else will."
> - Jack Welch

Taking Control of Your Week

Command

It's important to know that you control the command over your mental state in order to reach your full potential as an athlete. Catch yourself if you find your mind slipping into wavering thought patterns of "I can't" or "It's too much". Command a positive peak mental state when training and performing as an athlete. Here are some other practices you can use to control your level of command. The way you train, practice, hold yourself (presence), the food you eat and so on. Let yourself find new levels of command and write them down to strengthen your beliefs as an athlete.

Confidence

Confidence breeds belief in yourself as an athlete. If you are confident in what you do you show everyone else around that you believe in yourself and your abilities. Athletes need to apply confidence in everything they do. Confidence in their training, performance, execution, mental state, etc. Gain confidence by seizing control over your opportunities and application towards the area of athletics you are in. Try and apply this formula to help reach your athletic goal.

Opportunity + Ability + Preparation + Control + Confidence + Correct Application = Success

Competitiveness

An athlete's greatest competition is against themselves. Athletes need to compete to be their very best every day to help reach their ultimate athlete goal. Try to think of ways of competing beyond the game to raise your competitive mental state. Competing helps to raise your confidence and form a "can't lose", "hard-hitting", purposeful mindset. Compete and train with every bit of your mental and physical arsenal.

> "Confidence comes naturally with success. But, success comes only to those, who are confident."
> - Unknown

Taking Control of Your Week

Condition

Condition your mental and physical state of actions to form new heightened beliefs in yourself as an athlete. Stretch the boundaries of your conditioning mentally and physically. Truly see how much you can stand in training and in game performance. Try to condition yourself in a productive positive environment. Condition your mind to speed up or slow down time to your advantage. Condition your mind to find new levels of consciousness that will help you strengthen your game.

Coordinate

Coordinate your thoughts in order to coordinate your abilities, habits, and goals. Coordination heightens the athlete's training and performance by creating balance in the body, mind, and spirit. Coordinate your thoughts to condition the mind, body, and spirit to be the controlled, confident, committed competitor you want to be.

Communication

Athletes need to start with communication with themselves. Listen to what the athlete "you" is saying in order to help raise your level of awareness. Try to communicate to yourself in a positive, peak conceptual state. Forming positive communication behaviors will certainly help you to achieve your goals. By communicating with yourself, you will form better conversational habits with your coaches and trainers in order to help you gain information and feedback. You are what you communicate to others and yourself.

Composure

Compose your thoughts and actions in the manner that will help you become the athlete you want to be. If you're trying to get to a specific outcome in your training, try composing your thoughts towards that specific goal. Compose your thoughts in order to create a positive attitude and compose your actions to show the universe the positive person you are.

Taking Control of Your Week

Contribute

Contribution starts with the giving to others. You will get back in abundance what you give, so be relentless in your intent to give. In order to become a better athlete, give back through conversations and actions. Teach and coach others what you have learned along the way in your journey to your ultimate goal. Doing this will help strengthen your beliefs in yourself and strengthen your capabilities in achieving your ultimate goal of success.

Convert

Be honest with yourself. Know where you really stand in your knowledge and abilities. Seek clarity in your knowledge base. Not all training is the right training for you personally. Convert your thoughts to how you measure up to other athletes in your field and know exactly where you want to be. Convert your mind, body, and spirit to focus on real lasting change to the purpose of who you want to become. Convert your beliefs so you can convert to the new athlete you want to be. Navigate your own path to becoming a successful athlete by converting yourself to that path.

Champion

Once you have mastered the process of who you want to become in as an athlete, your limitless potential will set you on the path of championing your destiny. Once you do this you will achieve your desired level of results, helping you reach your ultimate goal. You must learn to champion the mind, body, and spirit in order to be a true champion.

"C" - On Your Own

Now that you have an idea and direction based upon the key C words we laid out, see if you can come up with an expanded list of C's or any other alpha key words to help you expand your knowledge base. These words will help you develop meaning on your own and will have a very personal definition and ownership for you as you define them. Doing this will strengthen the course you're on, getting to the end result you want.

Taking Control of Your Week

Current Strengths

Here is your opportunity to list out all the things you feel are going right. List out specific strengths as it pertains to training, performance, mental state, and so on. Knowing your strengths will help you focus on what's working and areas you might not need to spend more time on. Now go on, brag about yourself a bit.

> "Strength does not come from winning. Your struggles develop your strengths. When you go through hardships and decide not to surrender, that is strength." - Arnold Schwarzenegger

Current Self Rank

I added this in, not as a focal point, but as a measurement. Sometimes as an athlete it helps to see gains, and one way we can do that is by putting a number to it. My thought is that this will present some small knowledge to how your strength and efforts are relating to this relevant piece of being an athlete. From a score of 1 - 10 put the number in each week you feel fits with your athletic goals and efforts as a whole. Add this number in each week. This number will be a standard to live up to that you set for yourself.

> "Athletes in general are limited by two things. Their current level of understanding and their fear of the adjustments that has to happen"
> - Jason Beeding

Taking Control of Your Week

Things to work on

Successful athletes look back on each week in honesty and grade themselves on how they did. This is the time to really be truthful and honest about where you are as an athlete working towards your goal. How do you see your current state as it relates to your 6-month, 12-month and ultimate goal? List your training deficiencies, mental state problems and mechanical issues; basically, anything you see as limiting factors to work on the following week.

Weekly Reflections

Time to list any big victories you had during the week and areas you improved upon during the week. This will help you chart and track small wins each week in relation to getting where you want, your ultimate goal.

How I felt this week

Did you accomplish what you wrote down? How did you feel about your performance this week? Don't worry. There is no wrong or right answer here, it's more about you owning your process to help you be more aware of where you were at each given week. Not every week is going to be outstanding and not every week is going to be bad. These measures of feeling may give you some valuable insight as to how you prepared for your week and how you can prepare for the future. When you have outstanding weeks, look back at what you filled out on your weekly sheet. It may lead you to making some necessary adjustments.

Areas You Improved

List a few significant areas you improved on that week. These can be big or small it all matters to you and your improvement. They can be personal records in weight lifting or gains in throwing velocity. Any area you improved upon for the week.

Taking Control of Your Week

Monthly Review

I feel it's important to do a check-up on yourself after every 4-week period. Look at your entire month and define what worked and what didn't work for you. Just as you did for your weeks, but on a slightly bigger scale. By taking on your athletic goal in bites you will shrink the time it takes for you to accomplish it. You will want to measure your MRS each month. Be honest with yourself. If you had a bad month in terms of "intent", own that. The more honest you are with yourself the more you will understand the process and own the adjustments you need to make in the following month. The important thing is to complete the section. Remember if you don't write it down you are just renting your thoughts. Writing it down presents a form of commitment and ownership of your thoughts and accomplishments.

Success Notes

This is a free form page at the end of each 4-week period to free write any notes or thoughts you have or had during that period. Don't hold back here; write down your thoughts, feeling and ideas. Write down anything that comes to mind. This planner is for you and your success so there is nothing to leave out. You may want to come back later and reference these feelings or notes for future use.

> "Success isn't something that just happens, success is learned, success is practiced and then it is shared." - Sparky Anderson

Control Your Day [S.M.A.R.T]

Specific | **M**easurable | **A**chievable | **R**elevant | **T**ime Bound

Monday

| Goals | Actions | Workouts | Food | Water | **Mood Meter** |

_____

Tuesday

| Goals | Actions | Workouts | Food | Water | **Mood Meter** |

_____

Wednesday

| Goals | Actions | Workouts | Food | Water | **Mood Meter** |

_____

Thursday

| Goals | Actions | Workouts | Food | Water | **Mood Meter** |

_____

Friday

| Goals | Actions | Workouts | Food | Water | **Mood Meter** |

_____

Saturday

| Goals | Actions | Workouts | Food | Water | **Mood Meter** |

_____

Sunday

| Goals | Actions | Workouts | Food | Water | **Mood Meter** |

_____

Control Your Week of Success

"Hard work beats talent when talent doesn't work hard." – Tim Notke

Date:	Weekly Goals	Week#

_____
_____
_____
_____

Training Days	Weekly Drills	Power C's To Reflect On
Monday: _____	_____	**Used to help you retain focus to achieve your goals**
Tuesday: _____	_____	
Wednesday: _____	_____	_____
Thursday: _____	_____	_____
Friday: _____	_____	_____
Saturday: _____	_____	_____
Sunday: _____		_____
Notes: _____		_____
_____		_____
_____		

Current Strengths: Current Self Rank: _____

Areas that you feel are working well for you. Can be max lifts, mechanics, mental strengths, etc.

_____
_____
_____

Things to work on:

Areas you feel need to be improved upon in order to reach your goals.

_____
_____
_____

Weekly Reflections

Big Victories This Week   Areas You Improved

_____   _____
_____   _____
_____   _____

How I felt this week:
Outstanding | Excellent | Great | Good | Bad

Control Your Week of Success

"It's hard to beat a person who never gives up." - Babe Ruth

Date:	Weekly Goals	Week#

_____
_____
_____
_____

Training Days	Weekly Drills	Power C's To Reflect On
Monday: _____	_____	**Used to help you retain focus to achieve your goals**
Tuesday: _____	_____	
Wednesday: _____	_____	_____
Thursday: _____	_____	_____
Friday: _____	_____	_____
Saturday: _____		_____
Sunday: _____		_____
Notes: _____		_____
_____		_____
_____		

Current Strengths: Current Self Rank: _____

Areas that you feel are working well for you. Can be max lifts, mechanics, mental strengths, etc.

_____
_____
_____

Things to work on:

Areas you feel need to be improved upon in order to reach your goals.

_____
_____
_____

Weekly Reflections

Big Victories This Week   Areas You Improved

_____   _____
_____   _____
_____   _____

How I felt this week:
Outstanding | Excellent | Great | Good | Bad

Control Your Week of Success

"The harder the battle, the sweeter the victory." - Les Brown

Date:	Weekly Goals	Week#

_____
_____
_____
_____

Training Days	Weekly Drills	Power C's To Reflect On
Monday: _____	_____	**Used to help you retain focus to achieve your goals**
Tuesday: _____	_____	
Wednesday: _____	_____	_____
Thursday: _____	_____	_____
Friday: _____	_____	_____
Saturday: _____	_____	_____
Sunday: _____		_____
Notes: _____		_____
_____		_____
_____		

Current Strengths: Current Self Rank: _____

Areas that you feel are working well for you. Can be max lifts, mechanics, mental strengths, etc.

_____
_____
_____

Things to work on:

Areas you feel need to be improved upon in order to reach your goals.

_____
_____
_____

Weekly Reflections

Big Victories This Week   Areas You Improved

_____   _____
_____   _____
_____   _____

How I felt this week:
Outstanding | Excellent | Great | Good | Bad

Control Your Week of Success

"Never say never because limits, like fears, are often just illusion." - Michael Jordan

Date:	Weekly Goals	Week#

_____

Training Days	Weekly Drills	Power C's To Reflect On
Monday: _____	_____	**Used to help you retain focus to achieve your goals**
Tuesday: _____	_____	
Wednesday: _____	_____	_____
Thursday: _____	_____	_____
Friday: _____	_____	_____
Saturday: _____	_____	_____
Sunday: _____		_____
Notes: _____		_____

Current Strengths: Current Self Rank: _____

Areas that you feel are working well for you. Can be max lifts, mechanics, mental strengths, etc.

_____

Things to work on:

Areas you feel need to be improved upon in order to reach your goals.

_____

Weekly Reflections

Big Victories This Week   **Areas You Improved**

How I felt this week:
Outstanding | Excellent | Great | Good | Bad

Monthly Review

Super Successes:

These are targeted success you have had this month. Triumphs that will help you reach your goal.

_____

_____

_____

How Will These Super Successes Help You Reach Your One-year Goal?

_____

_____

_____

_____

Biggest Difficulties:

What were some difficulties this month that stood in your way of accomplishing more?

_____

_____

_____

_____   _____

How Can You Improve Next Month?

List any improvements you could have made looking back?

_____

_____

_____

_____

What Did You Learn From The Previous Month?

List major takeaways.

_____

_____

_____

Who Could Have Helped You Last Month?

List individuals that you know that could have helped you last month and see if you can ask them for advice heading into your new month.

_____

_____

I Had Relentless Intent This Month: Y/N
I Accomplished My Month with Massive Purpose: Y/N
I Was a Super Success This Month: Y / N

Success Notes

Control Your Day [S.M.A.R.T]

Specific | Measurable | Achievable | Relevant | Time Bound

Monday   **Mood Meter**
Goals   Actions   Workouts   Food   Water

Tuesday   **Mood Meter**
Goals   Actions   Workouts   Food   Water

Wednesday   **Mood Meter**
Goals   Actions   Workouts   Food   Water

Thursday   **Mood Meter**
Goals   Actions   Workouts   Food   Water

Friday   **Mood Meter**
Goals   Actions   Workouts   Food   Water

Saturday   **Mood Meter**
Goals   Actions   Workouts   Food   Water

Sunday   **Mood Meter**
Goals   Actions   Workouts   Food   Water

Control Your Week of Success

"You miss 100% of the shots you don't take." - Wayne Gretzky

Date:	Weekly Goals	Week#

_____

_____

_____

_____

Training Days	Weekly Drills	Power C's To Reflect On
Monday: _____	_____	**Used to help you retain focus to achieve your goals**
Tuesday: _____	_____	
Wednesday: _____	_____	_____
Thursday: _____	_____	_____
Friday: _____	_____	_____
Saturday: _____	_____	_____
Sunday: _____		_____
Notes: _____		_____
_____		_____
_____		

Current Strengths: Current Self Rank: _____

Areas that you feel are working well for you. Can be max lifts, mechanics, mental strengths, etc.

_____

_____

_____

Things to work on:

Areas you feel need to be improved upon in order to reach your goals.

_____

_____

_____

Weekly Reflections

Big Victories This Week   Areas You Improved

_____   _____

_____   _____

_____   _____

How I felt this week:
Outstanding | Excellent | Great | Good | Bad

Control Your Week of Success

"Today, you have 100% of your life left." - Tom Landry

Date:	Weekly Goals	Week#

_____
_____
_____
_____

Training Days	Weekly Drills	Power C's To Reflect On
Monday: _____	_____	**Used to help you retain focus to achieve your goals**
Tuesday: _____	_____	
Wednesday: _____	_____	_____
Thursday: _____	_____	_____
Friday: _____	_____	_____
Saturday: _____	_____	_____
Sunday: _____		_____
Notes: _____		_____
_____		_____
_____		

Current Strengths: Current Self Rank: _____

Areas that you feel are working well for you. Can be max lifts, mechanics, mental strengths, etc.

_____
_____
_____

Things to work on:

Areas you feel need to be improved upon in order to reach your goals.

_____
_____
_____

Weekly Reflections

Big Victories This Week   Areas You Improved

_____   _____
_____   _____
_____   _____

How I felt this week:
Outstanding | Excellent | Great | Good | Bad

Control Your Week of Success

"You have to expect things of yourself before you can do them." - Michael Jordan

Date:	Weekly Goals	Week#

_____
_____
_____
_____

Training Days	Weekly Drills	Power C's To Reflect On
Monday: _____	_____	**Used to help you retain focus to achieve your goals**
Tuesday: _____	_____	_____
Wednesday: _____	_____	_____
Thursday: _____	_____	_____
Friday: _____	_____	_____
Saturday: _____	_____	_____
Sunday: _____		_____
Notes: _____		_____
_____		
_____		

Current Strengths: Current Self Rank: _____

Areas that you feel are working well for you. Can be max lifts, mechanics, mental strengths, etc.

_____
_____
_____

Things to work on:

Areas you feel need to be improved upon in order to reach your goals.

_____
_____
_____

Weekly Reflections

Big Victories This Week   Areas You Improved

_____   _____
_____   _____
_____   _____

How I felt this week:
Outstanding | Excellent | Great | Good | Bad

Control Your Week of Success

"Winning isn't everything, but wanting to win is." - Vince Lombardi

Date:	Weekly Goals	Week#

Training Days
Monday: _____
Tuesday: _____
Wednesday: _____
Thursday: _____
Friday: _____
Saturday: _____
Sunday: _____
Notes: _____
_____
_____

Weekly Drills
_____
_____
_____
_____
_____
_____

Power C's To Reflect On
Used to help you retain focus to achieve your goals

_____
_____
_____
_____
_____
_____

Current Strengths: Current Self Rank: _____

Areas that you feel are working well for you. Can be max lifts, mechanics, mental strengths, etc.

_____
_____
_____

Things to work on:

Areas you feel need to be improved upon in order to reach your goals.

_____
_____
_____

Weekly Reflections

Big Victories This Week   Areas You Improved

_____   _____
_____   _____
_____   _____

How I felt this week:
Outstanding | Excellent | Great | Good | Bad

Monthly Review

Super Successes:

These are targeted success you have had this month. Triumphs that will help you reach your goal.

_____
_____
_____

How Will These Super Successes Help You Reach Your One-year Goal?

_____
_____
_____
_____

Biggest Difficulties:

What were some difficulties this month that stood in your way of accomplishing more?

_____
_____
_____
_____   _____

How Can You Improve Next Month?

List any improvements you could have made looking back?

_____
_____   _____
_____
_____

What Did You Learn From The Previous Month?

List major takeaways.

_____
_____
_____

Who Could Have Helped You Last Month?

List individuals that you know that could have helped you last month and see if you can ask them for advice heading into your new month.

_____
_____

I Had Relentless Intent This Month: Y/N
I Accomplished My Month with Massive Purpose: Y/N
I Was a Super Success This Month: Y / N

Success Notes

Control Your Day [S.M.A.R.T]

Specific | Measurable | Achievable | Relevant | Time Bound

Monday
| | | | | | **Mood Meter** |
| Goals | Actions | Workouts | Food | Water | | | | | | | | | |

_____
_____
_____

Tuesday
| | | | | | **Mood Meter** |
| Goals | Actions | Workouts | Food | Water | | | | | | | | | |

_____
_____
_____

Wednesday
| | | | | | **Mood Meter** |
| Goals | Actions | Workouts | Food | Water | | | | | | | | | |

_____
_____
_____

Thursday
| | | | | | **Mood Meter** |
| Goals | Actions | Workouts | Food | Water | | | | | | | | | |

_____
_____
_____

Friday
| | | | | | **Mood Meter** |
| Goals | Actions | Workouts | Food | Water | | | | | | | | | |

_____
_____
_____

Saturday
| | | | | | **Mood Meter** |
| Goals | Actions | Workouts | Food | Water | | | | | | | | | |

_____
_____
_____

Sunday
| | | | | | **Mood Meter** |
| Goals | Actions | Workouts | Food | Water | | | | | | | | | |

_____
_____
_____

Control Your Week of Success

"There may be people that have more talent than you, but there's no excuse for anyone to work harder than you do." - Derek Jeter

Date:	Weekly Goals	Week#

_____

Training Days	Weekly Drills	Power C's To Reflect On
Monday: _____	_____	**Used to help you retain focus to achieve your goals**
Tuesday: _____	_____	
Wednesday: _____	_____	_____
Thursday: _____	_____	_____
Friday: _____	_____	_____
Saturday: _____	_____	_____
Sunday: _____		_____
Notes: _____		_____
_____		

Current Strengths: Current Self Rank: _____

Areas that you feel are working well for you. Can be max lifts, mechanics, mental strengths, etc.

_____
_____
_____

Things to work on:

Areas you feel need to be improved upon in order to reach your goals.

_____
_____
_____

Weekly Reflections

Big Victories This Week   Areas You Improved

_____   _____
_____   _____
_____   _____

How I felt this week:
Outstanding | Excellent | Great | Good | Bad

Control Your Week of Success

"I became a good pitcher when I stopped trying to make them miss the ball and started trying to make them hit it." - Sandy Koufax

Date:	Weekly Goals	Week#

_____
_____
_____
_____

Training Days	Weekly Drills	Power C's To Reflect On
Monday: _____	_____	**Used to help you retain focus to achieve your goals**
Tuesday: _____	_____	
Wednesday: _____	_____	_____
Thursday: _____	_____	_____
Friday: _____	_____	_____
Saturday: _____	_____	_____
Sunday: _____		_____
Notes: _____		_____
_____		_____
_____		

Current Strengths: Current Self Rank: _____

Areas that you feel are working well for you. Can be max lifts, mechanics, mental strengths, etc.

_____
_____
_____

Things to work on:

Areas you feel need to be improved upon in order to reach your goals.

_____
_____
_____

Weekly Reflections

Big Victories This Week   Areas You Improved

_____   _____
_____   _____
_____   _____

How I felt this week:
Outstanding | Excellent | Great | Good | Bad

Control Your Week of Success

"When you've got something to prove, there's nothing greater than a challenge." - Terry Bradshaw

Date:	Weekly Goals	Week#

_____
_____
_____
_____

Training Days	Weekly Drills	Power C's To Reflect On
Monday: _____	_____	**Used to help you retain focus to achieve your goals**
Tuesday: _____	_____	
Wednesday: _____	_____	_____
Thursday: _____	_____	_____
Friday: _____	_____	_____
Saturday: _____	_____	_____
Sunday: _____		_____
Notes: _____		_____
_____		

Current Strengths: Current Self Rank: _____

Areas that you feel are working well for you. Can be max lifts, mechanics, mental strengths, etc.

_____
_____
_____

Things to work on:

Areas you feel need to be improved upon in order to reach your goals.

_____
_____
_____

Weekly Reflections

Big Victories This Week   Areas You Improved

_____   _____
_____   _____
_____   _____

How I felt this week:
Outstanding | Excellent | Great | Good | Bad

Control Your Week of Success

"If you can't outplay them, outwork them." - Ben Hogan

Date:	Weekly Goals	Week#

_____

Training Days	Weekly Drills	Power C's To Reflect On
Monday: _____	_____	**Used to help you retain focus to achieve your goals**
Tuesday: _____	_____	
Wednesday: _____	_____	_____
Thursday: _____	_____	_____
Friday: _____	_____	_____
Saturday: _____	_____	_____
Sunday: _____		_____
Notes: _____		_____
_____		_____
_____		

Current Strengths: Current Self Rank: _____

Areas that you feel are working well for you. Can be max lifts, mechanics, mental strengths, etc.

_____
_____
_____

Things to work on:

Areas you feel need to be improved upon in order to reach your goals.

_____
_____
_____

Weekly Reflections

Big Victories This Week   Areas You Improved

_____   _____

_____   _____

_____   _____

How I felt this week:
Outstanding | Excellent | Great | Good | Bad

Monthly Review

Super Successes:

These are targeted success you have had this month. Triumphs that will help you reach your goal.

_____
_____
_____

How Will These Super Successes Help You Reach Your One-year Goal?

_____
_____
_____
_____

Biggest Difficulties:

What were some difficulties this month that stood in your way of accomplishing more?

_____
_____
_____
_____   _____

How Can You Improve Next Month?

List any improvements you could have made looking back?

_____
_____
_____
_____

What Did You Learn From The Previous Month?

List major takeaways.

_____
_____
_____

Who Could Have Helped You Last Month?

List individuals that you know that could have helped you last month and see if you can ask them for advice heading into your new month.

_____
_____

I Had Relentless Intent This Month: Y/N
I Accomplished My Month with Massive Purpose: Y/N
I Was a Super Success This Month: Y / N

Success Notes

Control Your Day [S.M.A.R.T]

Specific | **M**easurable | **A**chievable | **R**elevant | Time Bound

Monday   **Mood Meter**
Goals   Actions   Workouts   Food   Water | | | | | | | | |

___

Tuesday   **Mood Meter**
Goals   Actions   Workouts   Food   Water | | | | | | | | |

___

Wednesday   **Mood Meter**
Goals   Actions   Workouts   Food   Water | | | | | | | | |

___

Thursday   **Mood Meter**
Goals   Actions   Workouts   Food   Water | | | | | | | | |

___

Friday   **Mood Meter**
Goals   Actions   Workouts   Food   Water | | | | | | | | |

___

Saturday   **Mood Meter**
Goals   Actions   Workouts   Food   Water | | | | | | | | |

___

Sunday   **Mood Meter**
Goals   Actions   Workouts   Food   Water | | | | | | | | |

Control Your Week of Success

"Most people never run far enough on their first wind to find out they've got a second." -
William James

Date:	Weekly Goals	Week#

_____

Training Days	Weekly Drills	Power C's To Reflect On
Monday: _____	_____	**Used to help you retain focus to achieve your goals**
Tuesday: _____	_____	
Wednesday: _____	_____	_____
Thursday: _____	_____	_____
Friday: _____	_____	_____
Saturday: _____	_____	_____
Sunday: _____		_____
Notes: _____		_____
_____		
_____		

Current Strengths: Current Self Rank: _____

Areas that you feel are working well for you. Can be max lifts, mechanics, mental strengths, etc.

_____

Things to work on:

Areas you feel need to be improved upon in order to reach your goals.

_____

Weekly Reflections

Big Victories This Week   Areas You Improved

_____   _____

_____   _____

_____   _____

How I felt this week:
Outstanding | Excellent | Great | Good | Bad

Control Your Week of Success

"I've failed over and over and over again in my life. And that is why I succeed."
- Michael Jordan

Date:	Weekly Goals	Week#

_____
_____
_____
_____

Training Days	Weekly Drills	Power C's To Reflect On
Monday: _____	_____	**Used to help you retain focus to achieve your goals**
Tuesday: _____	_____	
Wednesday: _____	_____	_____
Thursday: _____	_____	_____
Friday: _____	_____	_____
Saturday: _____	_____	_____
Sunday: _____		_____
Notes: _____		_____
_____		_____
_____		

Current Strengths: Current Self Rank: _____

Areas that you feel are working well for you. Can be max lifts, mechanics, mental strengths, etc.

_____
_____
_____

Things to work on:

Areas you feel need to be improved upon in order to reach your goals.

_____
_____
_____

Weekly Reflections

Big Victories This Week   Areas You Improved

_____   _____
_____   _____
_____   _____

How I felt this week:
Outstanding | Excellent | Great | Good | Bad

Control Your Week of Success

"It's not whether you get knocked down; it's whether you get up." - Vince Lombardi

Date:	Weekly Goals	Week#

_____

_____

_____

_____

Training Days	Weekly Drills	Power C's To Reflect On
Monday: _____	_____	**Used to help you retain focus to achieve your goals**
Tuesday: _____	_____	
Wednesday: _____	_____	_____
Thursday: _____	_____	_____
Friday: _____	_____	_____
Saturday: _____	_____	_____
Sunday: _____		_____
Notes: _____		_____
_____		_____
_____		

Current Strengths: Current Self Rank: _____

Areas that you feel are working well for you. Can be max lifts, mechanics, mental strengths, etc.

_____

_____

_____

Things to work on:

Areas you feel need to be improved upon in order to reach your goals.

_____

_____

_____

Weekly Reflections

Big Victories This Week   Areas You Improved

_____   _____

_____   _____

_____   _____

How I felt this week:
Outstanding | Excellent | Great | Good | Bad

Control Your Week of Success

"Do you know what my favorite part of the game is? The opportunity to play."
- Mike Singletary

Date:	Weekly Goals	Week#

_____

Training Days	Weekly Drills	Power C's To Reflect On
Monday: _____	_____	**Used to help you retain focus to achieve your goals**
Tuesday: _____	_____	
Wednesday: _____	_____	_____
Thursday: _____	_____	_____
Friday: _____	_____	_____
Saturday: _____	_____	_____
Sunday: _____		_____
Notes: _____		_____
_____		_____
_____		

Current Strengths: Current Self Rank: _____

Areas that you feel are working well for you. Can be max lifts, mechanics, mental strengths, etc.

_____
_____
_____

Things to work on:

Areas you feel need to be improved upon in order to reach your goals.

_____
_____
_____

Weekly Reflections

Big Victories This Week   Areas You Improved

_____   _____
_____   _____
_____   _____

How I felt this week:
Outstanding | Excellent | Great | Good | Bad

Monthly Review

Super Successes:

These are targeted success you have had this month. Triumphs that will help you reach your goal.

_____
_____
_____

How Will These Super Successes Help You Reach Your One-year Goal?

_____
_____
_____
_____

Biggest Difficulties:

What were some difficulties this month that stood in your way of accomplishing more?

_____
_____
_____
_____   _____

How Can You Improve Next Month?

List any improvements you could have made looking back?

_____
_____
_____
_____

What Did You Learn From The Previous Month?

List major takeaways.

_____
_____
_____

Who Could Have Helped You Last Month?

List individuals that you know that could have helped you last month and see if you can ask them for advice heading into your new month.

_____
_____

I Had Relentless Intent This Month: Y/N
I Accomplished My Month with Massive Purpose: Y/N
I Was a Super Success This Month: Y / N

Success Notes

Massive Purpose.   Relentless Intent.   Super Success.

Control Your Day [S.M.A.R.T]

Specific | Measurable | Achievable | Relevant | Time Bound

Monday

Goals   Actions   Workouts   Food   Water

Mood Meter

| | | | | | | | |

Tuesday

Goals   Actions   Workouts   Food   Water

Mood Meter

| | | | | | | | |

Wednesday

Goals   Actions   Workouts   Food   Water

Mood Meter

| | | | | | | | |

Thursday

Goals   Actions   Workouts   Food   Water

Mood Meter

| | | | | | | | |

Friday

Goals   Actions   Workouts   Food   Water

Mood Meter

| | | | | | | | |

Saturday

Goals   Actions   Workouts   Food   Water

Mood Meter

| | | | | | | | |

Sunday

Goals   Actions   Workouts   Food   Water

Mood Meter

| | | | | | | | |

Control Your Week of Success

"The more difficult the victory, the greater the happiness in winning." - Pele

Date:	Weekly Goals	Week#

_____
_____
_____
_____

Training Days	Weekly Drills	Power C's To Reflect On
Monday: _____	_____	**Used to help you retain focus to achieve your goals**
Tuesday: _____	_____	
Wednesday: _____	_____	_____
Thursday: _____	_____	_____
Friday: _____	_____	_____
Saturday: _____	_____	_____
Sunday: _____		_____
Notes: _____		_____
_____		
_____		

Current Strengths: Current Self Rank: _____

Areas that you feel are working well for you. Can be max lifts, mechanics, mental strengths, etc.

_____
_____
_____

Things to work on:

Areas you feel need to be improved upon in order to reach your goals.

_____
_____
_____

Weekly Reflections

Big Victories This Week   Areas You Improved

_____   _____
_____   _____
_____   _____

How I felt this week:
Outstanding | Excellent | Great | Good | Bad

Control Your Week of Success

"Nobody who ever gave his best regretted it." - George Halas

Date:	Weekly Goals	Week#

_____

_____

_____

_____

Training Days	Weekly Drills	Power C's To Reflect On
Monday: _____	_____	**Used to help you retain focus to achieve your goals**
Tuesday: _____	_____	
Wednesday: _____	_____	_____
Thursday: _____	_____	_____
Friday: _____	_____	_____
Saturday: _____	_____	_____
Sunday: _____		_____
Notes: _____		_____
_____		_____
_____		

Current Strengths: Current Self Rank: _____

Areas that you feel are working well for you. Can be max lifts, mechanics, mental strengths, etc.

_____

_____

_____

Things to work on:

Areas you feel need to be improved upon in order to reach your goals.

_____

_____

_____

Weekly Reflections

Big Victories This Week   Areas You Improved

_____   _____

_____   _____

_____   _____

How I felt this week:
Outstanding | Excellent | Great | Good | Bad

Control Your Week of Success

"If you can believe it, the mind can achieve it." - Ronnie Lott

Date:	Weekly Goals	Week#

_____
_____
_____
_____

Training Days	Weekly Drills	Power C's To Reflect On
Monday: _____	_____	**Used to help you retain focus to achieve your goals**
Tuesday: _____	_____	
Wednesday: _____	_____	_____
Thursday: _____	_____	_____
Friday: _____	_____	_____
Saturday: _____	_____	_____
Sunday: _____		_____
Notes: _____		_____
_____		_____

Current Strengths: Current Self Rank: _____

Areas that you feel are working well for you. Can be max lifts, mechanics, mental strengths, etc.

_____
_____
_____

Things to work on:

Areas you feel need to be improved upon in order to reach your goals.

_____
_____
_____

Weekly Reflections

Big Victories This Week   Areas You Improved

_____   _____
_____   _____
_____   _____

How I felt this week:
Outstanding | Excellent | Great | Good | Bad

Control Your Week of Success

"Without self-discipline, success is impossible, period." - Lou Holtz

Date:	Weekly Goals	Week#

_____

Training Days	Weekly Drills	Power C's To Reflect On
Monday: _____	_____	**Used to help you retain focus to achieve your goals**
Tuesday: _____	_____	
Wednesday: _____	_____	_____
Thursday: _____	_____	_____
Friday: _____	_____	_____
Saturday: _____	_____	_____
Sunday: _____		_____
Notes: _____		_____
_____		_____
_____		

Current Strengths: Current Self Rank: _____

Areas that you feel are working well for you. Can be max lifts, mechanics, mental strengths, etc.

_____
_____
_____

Things to work on:

Areas you feel need to be improved upon in order to reach your goals.

_____
_____
_____

Weekly Reflections

Big Victories This Week   Areas You Improved

_____   _____
_____   _____
_____   _____

How I felt this week:
Outstanding | Excellent | Great | Good | Bad

Monthly Review

Super Successes:

These are targeted success you have had this month. Triumphs that will help you reach your goal.

_____

_____

_____

How Will These Super Successes Help You Reach Your One-year Goal?

_____

_____

_____

_____

Biggest Difficulties:

What were some difficulties this month that stood in your way of accomplishing more?

_____

_____

_____

_____   _____

How Can You Improve Next Month?

List any improvements you could have made looking back?

_____

_____

_____

_____

What Did You Learn From The Previous Month?

List major takeaways.

_____

_____

_____

Who Could Have Helped You Last Month?

List individuals that you know that could have helped you last month and see if you can ask them for advice heading into your new month.

_____

_____

I Had Relentless Intent This Month: Y/N
I Accomplished My Month with Massive Purpose: Y/N
I Was a Super Success This Month: Y / N

Success Notes

Massive Purpose.   Relentless Intent.   Super Success.

Control Your Day [S.M.A.R.T]

Specific | Measurable | Achievable | Relevant | Time Bound

Monday

Goals	Actions	Workouts	Food	Water	Mood Meter

Tuesday

Goals	Actions	Workouts	Food	Water	Mood Meter

Wednesday

Goals	Actions	Workouts	Food	Water	Mood Meter

Thursday

Goals	Actions	Workouts	Food	Water	Mood Meter

Friday

Goals	Actions	Workouts	Food	Water	Mood Meter

Saturday

Goals	Actions	Workouts	Food	Water	Mood Meter

Sunday

Goals	Actions	Workouts	Food	Water	Mood Meter

Control Your Week of Success

"Make each day your masterpiece." - John Wooden

Date:	Weekly Goals	Week#

_____

_____

_____

_____

Training Days	Weekly Drills	Power C's To Reflect On
Monday: _____	_____	**Used to help you retain focus to achieve your goals**
Tuesday: _____	_____	
Wednesday: _____	_____	_____
Thursday: _____	_____	_____
Friday: _____	_____	_____
Saturday: _____	_____	_____
Sunday: _____		_____
Notes: _____		_____
_____		_____
_____		

Current Strengths: Current Self Rank: _____

Areas that you feel are working well for you. Can be max lifts, mechanics, mental strengths, etc.

_____

_____

_____

Things to work on:

Areas you feel need to be improved upon in order to reach your goals.

_____

_____

_____

Weekly Reflections

Big Victories This Week   Areas You Improved

_____   _____

_____   _____

_____   _____

How I felt this week:
Outstanding | Excellent | Great | Good | Bad

Massive Purpose.   Relentless Intent.   Super Success.

Control Your Week of Success

"If you aren't going all the way, why go at all?" - Joe Namath

Date:	Weekly Goals	Week#

_____
_____
_____
_____

Training Days	Weekly Drills	Power C's To Reflect On
Monday: _____	_____	**Used to help you retain focus to achieve your goals**
Tuesday: _____	_____	
Wednesday: _____	_____	_____
Thursday: _____	_____	_____
Friday: _____	_____	_____
Saturday: _____	_____	_____
Sunday: _____		_____
Notes: _____		_____
_____		_____

Current Strengths: Current Self Rank: _____

Areas that you feel are working well for you. Can be max lifts, mechanics, mental strengths, etc.

_____
_____
_____

Things to work on:

Areas you feel need to be improved upon in order to reach your goals.

_____
_____
_____

Weekly Reflections

Big Victories This Week   Areas You Improved

_____   _____
_____   _____
_____   _____

How I felt this week:
Outstanding | Excellent | Great | Good | Bad

Massive Purpose.   Relentless Intent.   Super Success.

Control Your Week of Success

"Do not let what you can not do interfere with what you can do." - John Wooden

Date:	Weekly Goals	Week#

_____
_____
_____

Training Days	Weekly Drills	Power C's To Reflect On
Monday: _____	_____	**Used to help you retain focus to achieve your goals**
Tuesday: _____	_____	
Wednesday: _____	_____	
Thursday: _____	_____	
Friday: _____	_____	
Saturday: _____	_____	
Sunday: _____		
Notes: _____		

Current Strengths: Current Self Rank: _____

Areas that you feel are working well for you. Can be max lifts, mechanics, mental strengths, etc.

_____
_____
_____

Things to work on:

Areas you feel need to be improved upon in order to reach your goals.

_____
_____
_____

Weekly Reflections

Big Victories This Week   Areas You Improved

_____   _____
_____   _____
_____   _____

How I felt this week:
Outstanding | Excellent | Great | Good | Bad

Control Your Week of Success

"A champion is someone who gets up when he can't." - Jack Dempsey

Date:	Weekly Goals	Week#

_____

_____

_____

_____

Training Days	Weekly Drills	Power C's To Reflect On
Monday: _____	_____	**Used to help you retain focus to achieve your goals**
Tuesday: _____	_____	
Wednesday: _____	_____	_____
Thursday: _____	_____	_____
Friday: _____	_____	_____
Saturday: _____	_____	_____
Sunday: _____		_____
Notes: _____		_____

Current Strengths: Current Self Rank: _____

Areas that you feel are working well for you. Can be max lifts, mechanics, mental strengths, etc.

_____

_____

_____

Things to work on:

Areas you feel need to be improved upon in order to reach your goals.

_____

_____

_____

Weekly Reflections

Big Victories This Week   Areas You Improved

_____   _____

_____   _____

_____   _____

How I felt this week:
Outstanding | Excellent | Great | Good | Bad

Monthly Review

Super Successes:

These are targeted success you have had this month. Triumphs that will help you reach your goal.

_____

_____

_____

How Will These Super Successes Help You Reach Your One-year Goal?

_____

_____

_____

_____

Biggest Difficulties:

What were some difficulties this month that stood in your way of accomplishing more?

_____

_____

_____

_____   _____

How Can You Improve Next Month?

List any improvements you could have made looking back?

_____

_____

_____

_____

What Did You Learn From The Previous Month?

List major takeaways.

_____

_____

_____

Who Could Have Helped You Last Month?

List individuals that you know that could have helped you last month and see if you can ask them for advice heading into your new month.

_____

_____

I Had Relentless Intent This Month: Y/N

I Accomplished My Month with Massive Purpose: Y/N

I Was a Super Success This Month: Y / N

Success Notes

Massive Purpose.   Relentless Intent.   Super Success.

Control Your Day [S.M.A.R.T]

Specific | **M**easurable | **A**chievable | **R**elevant | **T**ime Bound

Monday   **Mood Meter**
Goals   Actions   Workouts   Food   Water | | | | | | | | |

Tuesday   **Mood Meter**
Goals   Actions   Workouts   Food   Water | | | | | | | | |

Wednesday   **Mood Meter**
Goals   Actions   Workouts   Food   Water | | | | | | | | |

Thursday   **Mood Meter**
Goals   Actions   Workouts   Food   Water | | | | | | | | |

Friday   **Mood Meter**
Goals   Actions   Workouts   Food   Water | | | | | | | | |

Saturday   **Mood Meter**
Goals   Actions   Workouts   Food   Water | | | | | | | | |

Sunday   **Mood Meter**
Goals   Actions   Workouts   Food   Water | | | | | | | | |

Control Your Week of Success

"It ain't over 'til it's over." - Yogi Berra

Date:	Weekly Goals	Week#

_____
_____
_____
_____

Training Days	Weekly Drills	Power C's To Reflect On
Monday: _____	_____	**Used to help you retain focus to achieve your goals**
Tuesday: _____	_____	
Wednesday: _____	_____	_____
Thursday: _____	_____	_____
Friday: _____	_____	_____
Saturday: _____		_____
Sunday: _____		_____
Notes: _____		_____
_____		
_____		

Current Strengths: Current Self Rank: _____

Areas that you feel are working well for you. Can be max lifts, mechanics, mental strengths, etc.

_____
_____
_____

Things to work on:

Areas you feel need to be improved upon in order to reach your goals.

_____
_____
_____

Weekly Reflections

Big Victories This Week   Areas You Improved

_____   _____
_____   _____
_____   _____

How I felt this week:
Outstanding | Excellent | Great | Good | Bad

Control Your Week of Success

"Winners never quit and quitters never win." - Vince Lombardi

Date:	Weekly Goals	Week#

_____

_____

_____

_____

Training Days	Weekly Drills	Power C's To Reflect On
Monday: _____	_____	**Used to help you retain focus to achieve your goals**
Tuesday: _____	_____	
Wednesday: _____	_____	
Thursday: _____	_____	_____
Friday: _____	_____	_____
Saturday: _____	_____	_____
Sunday: _____		_____
Notes: _____		_____
_____		_____
_____		

Current Strengths: Current Self Rank: _____

Areas that you feel are working well for you. Can be max lifts, mechanics, mental strengths, etc.

_____

_____

_____

Things to work on:

Areas you feel need to be improved upon in order to reach your goals.

_____

_____

_____

Weekly Reflections

Big Victories This Week   Areas You Improved

_____   _____

_____   _____

_____   _____

How I felt this week:
Outstanding | Excellent | Great | Good | Bad

Control Your Week of Success

"One man practicing sportsmanship is far better than a hundred teaching it."
- Knute Rockne

Date:	Weekly Goals	Week#

_____

_____

_____

_____

Training Days	Weekly Drills	Power C's To Reflect On
Monday: _____	_____	**Used to help you retain focus to achieve your goals**
Tuesday: _____	_____	
Wednesday: _____	_____	_____
Thursday: _____	_____	_____
Friday: _____	_____	_____
Saturday: _____	_____	_____
Sunday: _____	_____	_____
Notes: _____		_____
_____		
_____		

Current Strengths: Current Self Rank: _____

Areas that you feel are working well for you. Can be max lifts, mechanics, mental strengths, etc.

_____

_____

_____

Things to work on:

Areas you feel need to be improved upon in order to reach your goals.

_____

_____

_____

Weekly Reflections

Big Victories This Week   Areas You Improved

_____   _____

_____   _____

_____   _____

How I felt this week:
Outstanding | Excellent | Great | Good | Bad

Control Your Week of Success

"Success is where preparation and opportunity meet." - Bobby Unser

Date:	Weekly Goals	Week#

_____

_____

_____

_____

Training Days	Weekly Drills	Power C's To Reflect On
Monday: _____	_____	**Used to help you retain focus to achieve your goals**
Tuesday: _____	_____	
Wednesday: _____	_____	_____
Thursday: _____	_____	_____
Friday: _____	_____	_____
Saturday: _____		_____
Sunday: _____		_____
Notes: _____		_____
_____		_____
_____		

Current Strengths: Current Self Rank: _____

Areas that you feel are working well for you. Can be max lifts, mechanics, mental strengths, etc.

_____

_____

_____

Things to work on:

Areas you feel need to be improved upon in order to reach your goals.

_____

_____

_____

Weekly Reflections

Big Victories This Week   Areas You Improved

_____   _____

_____   _____

_____   _____

How I felt this week:
Outstanding | Excellent | Great | Good | Bad

Monthly Review

Super Successes:

These are targeted success you have had this month. Triumphs that will help you reach your goal.

_____
_____
_____

How Will These Super Successes Help You Reach Your One-year Goal?

_____
_____
_____
_____

Biggest Difficulties:

What were some difficulties this month that stood in your way of accomplishing more?

_____
_____
_____
_____   _____

How Can You Improve Next Month?

List any improvements you could have made looking back?

_____
_____
_____
_____

What Did You Learn From The Previous Month?

List major takeaways.

_____
_____
_____

Who Could Have Helped You Last Month?

List individuals that you know that could have helped you last month and see if you can ask them for advice heading into your new month.

_____
_____

I Had Relentless Intent This Month: Y/N
I Accomplished My Month with Massive Purpose: Y/N
I Was a Super Success This Month: Y / N

Success Notes

Massive Purpose.   Relentless Intent.   Super Success.

Control Your Day [S.M.A.R.T]

Specific | Measurable | Achievable | Relevant | Time Bound

Monday   **Mood Meter**

Goals   Actions   Workouts   Food   Water | | | | | | | |

_____

_____

_____

Tuesday   **Mood Meter**

Goals   Actions   Workouts   Food   Water | | | | | | | |

_____

_____

_____

Wednesday   **Mood Meter**

Goals   Actions   Workouts   Food   Water | | | | | | | |

_____

_____

_____

Thursday   **Mood Meter**

Goals   Actions   Workouts   Food   Water | | | | | | | |

_____

_____

_____

Friday   **Mood Meter**

Goals   Actions   Workouts   Food   Water | | | | | | | |

_____

_____

_____

Saturday   **Mood Meter**

Goals   Actions   Workouts   Food   Water | | | | | | | |

_____

_____

_____

Sunday   **Mood Meter**

Goals   Actions   Workouts   Food   Water | | | | | | | |

_____

_____

_____

Control Your Week of Success

"In baseball and in business, there are three types of people. Those who make it happen, those who watch it happen, and those who wonder what happened." - Tommy Lasorda

Date:	Weekly Goals	Week#

_____
_____
_____
_____

Training Days	Weekly Drills	Power C's To Reflect On
Monday: _____	_____	**Used to help you retain focus to achieve your goals**
Tuesday: _____	_____	
Wednesday: _____	_____	_____
Thursday: _____	_____	_____
Friday: _____	_____	_____
Saturday: _____	_____	_____
Sunday: _____		_____
Notes: _____		_____
_____		_____
_____		

Current Strengths: **Current Self Rank: _____**

Areas that you feel are working well for you. Can be max lifts, mechanics, mental strengths, etc.

_____
_____
_____

Things to work on:

Areas you feel need to be improved upon in order to reach your goals.

_____
_____
_____

Weekly Reflections

Big Victories This Week   **Areas You Improved**

_____   _____
_____   _____
_____   _____

How I felt this week:
Outstanding | Excellent | Great | Good | Bad

Control Your Week of Success

"Champions keep playing until they get it right." - Billie Jean King

Date:	Weekly Goals	Week#

_____
_____
_____
_____

Training Days	Weekly Drills	Power C's To Reflect On
Monday: _____	_____	**Used to help you retain focus to achieve your goals**
Tuesday: _____	_____	_____
Wednesday: _____	_____	_____
Thursday: _____	_____	_____
Friday: _____	_____	_____
Saturday: _____	_____	_____
Sunday: _____		_____
Notes: _____		_____
_____		
_____		

Current Strengths: Current Self Rank: _____

Areas that you feel are working well for you. Can be max lifts, mechanics, mental strengths, etc.

_____
_____
_____

Things to work on:

Areas you feel need to be improved upon in order to reach your goals.

_____
_____
_____

Weekly Reflections

Big Victories This Week   Areas You Improved

_____   _____
_____   _____
_____   _____

How I felt this week:
Outstanding | Excellent | Great | Good | Bad

Control Your Week of Success

"It isn't the mountains ahead to climb that wear you out; it's the pebble in your shoe."
- Muhammad Ali

Date:	Weekly Goals	Week#

_____

Training Days	Weekly Drills	Power C's To Reflect On
Monday: _____	_____	**Used to help you retain focus to achieve your goals**
Tuesday: _____	_____	
Wednesday: _____	_____	_____
Thursday: _____	_____	_____
Friday: _____	_____	_____
Saturday: _____	_____	_____
Sunday: _____		_____
Notes: _____		_____
_____		_____
_____		

Current Strengths: Current Self Rank: _____

Areas that you feel are working well for you. Can be max lifts, mechanics, mental strengths, etc.

_____
_____
_____

Things to work on:

Areas you feel need to be improved upon in order to reach your goals.

_____
_____
_____

Weekly Reflections

Big Victories This Week   Areas You Improved

_____   _____
_____   _____
_____   _____

How I felt this week:
Outstanding | Excellent | Great | Good | Bad

Control Your Week of Success

"You can't put a limit on anything. The more you dream, the farther you get."
- Michael Phelps

Date:	Weekly Goals	Week#

_____
_____
_____
_____

Training Days
Monday: _____
Tuesday: _____
Wednesday: _____
Thursday: _____
Friday: _____
Saturday: _____
Sunday: _____
Notes: _____
_____
_____

Weekly Drills
_____
_____
_____
_____
_____

Power C's To Reflect On
Used to help you retain focus to achieve your goals
_____
_____
_____
_____
_____

Current Strengths: Current Self Rank: _____

Areas that you feel are working well for you. Can be max lifts, mechanics, mental strengths, etc.

_____
_____
_____

Things to work on:

Areas you feel need to be improved upon in order to reach your goals.

_____
_____
_____

Weekly Reflections

Big Victories This Week   Areas You Improved

_____   _____
_____   _____
_____   _____

How I felt this week:
Outstanding | Excellent | Great | Good | Bad

Monthly Review

Super Successes:

These are targeted success you have had this month. Triumphs that will help you reach your goal.

_____
_____
_____

How Will These Super Successes Help You Reach Your One-year Goal?

_____
_____
_____
_____

Biggest Difficulties:

What were some difficulties this month that stood in your way of accomplishing more?

_____
_____
_____
_____   _____

How Can You Improve Next Month?

List any improvements you could have made looking back?

_____
_____
_____
_____

What Did You Learn From The Previous Month?

List major takeaways.

_____
_____
_____

Who Could Have Helped You Last Month?

List individuals that you know that could have helped you last month and see if you can ask them for advice heading into your new month.

_____
_____

I Had Relentless Intent This Month: Y/N
I Accomplished My Month with Massive Purpose: Y/N
I Was a Super Success This Month: Y / N

Success Notes

Control Your Day [S.M.A.R.T]
Specific | Measurable | Achievable | Relevant | Time Bound

Monday   **Mood Meter**

Goals	Actions	Workouts	Food	Water									

Tuesday   **Mood Meter**

Goals	Actions	Workouts	Food	Water									

Wednesday   **Mood Meter**

Goals	Actions	Workouts	Food	Water									

Thursday   **Mood Meter**

Goals	Actions	Workouts	Food	Water									

Friday   **Mood Meter**

Goals	Actions	Workouts	Food	Water									

Saturday   **Mood Meter**

Goals	Actions	Workouts	Food	Water									

Sunday   **Mood Meter**

Goals	Actions	Workouts	Food	Water									

Control Your Week of Success

"Always make a total effort, even when the odds are against you." - Arnold Palmer

Date:	Weekly Goals	Week#

Training Days	Weekly Drills	Power C's To Reflect On
Monday: _____	_____	**Used to help you retain focus to achieve your goals**
Tuesday: _____	_____	
Wednesday: _____	_____	_____
Thursday: _____	_____	_____
Friday: _____	_____	_____
Saturday: _____	_____	_____
Sunday: _____		_____
Notes: _____		_____

Current Strengths:　　　　　　　　　　　**Current Self Rank: _____**

Areas that you feel are working well for you. Can be max lifts, mechanics, mental strengths, etc.

_____

_____

_____

Things to work on:

Areas you feel need to be improved upon in order to reach your goals.

_____

_____

_____

Weekly Reflections

Big Victories This Week　　　　　　　　**Areas You Improved**

_____　　　　　　　　_____

_____　　　　　　　　_____

_____　　　　　　　　_____

How I felt this week:
Outstanding | Excellent | Great | Good | Bad

Control Your Week of Success

"Winning is not a sometime thing, it is an all the time thing. You don't do things right once in a while. You do them right all the time." - Vince Lombardi

Date:	Weekly Goals	Week#

_____

_____

_____

Training Days	Weekly Drills	Power C's To Reflect On
Monday: _____	_____	**Used to help you retain focus to achieve your goals**
Tuesday: _____	_____	
Wednesday: _____	_____	_____
Thursday: _____	_____	_____
Friday: _____	_____	_____
Saturday: _____	_____	_____
Sunday: _____		_____
Notes: _____		_____
_____		
_____		

Current Strengths: Current Self Rank: _____

Areas that you feel are working well for you. Can be max lifts, mechanics, mental strengths, etc.

_____

_____

_____

Things to work on:

Areas you feel need to be improved upon in order to reach your goals.

_____

_____

_____

Weekly Reflections

Big Victories This Week   Areas You Improved

_____   _____

_____   _____

_____   _____

How I felt this week:
Outstanding | Excellent | Great | Good | Bad

Control Your Week of Success

"I'd like to thank everyone who voted for me. And the one guy who didn't vote for me, thank you, too" - Shaquille O'Neal

Date:	Weekly Goals	Week#

_____

Training Days	Weekly Drills	Power C's To Reflect On
Monday: _____	_____	**Used to help you retain focus to achieve your goals**
Tuesday: _____	_____	
Wednesday: _____	_____	_____
Thursday: _____	_____	_____
Friday: _____	_____	_____
Saturday: _____	_____	_____
Sunday: _____		_____
Notes: _____		_____

Current Strengths: Current Self Rank: _____

Areas that you feel are working well for you. Can be max lifts, mechanics, mental strengths, etc.

_____

Things to work on:

Areas you feel need to be improved upon in order to reach your goals.

_____

Weekly Reflections

Big Victories This Week   Areas You Improved

How I felt this week:
Outstanding | Excellent | Great | Good | Bad

Control Your Week of Success

"It's not the will to win that matters - Everyone has that. It's the will to prepare to win that matters." - Paul "Bear" Bryant

Date:	Weekly Goals	Week#

Training Days	Weekly Drills	Power C's To Reflect On
Monday: _____	_____	**Used to help you retain focus to achieve your goals**
Tuesday: _____	_____	
Wednesday: _____	_____	
Thursday: _____	_____	
Friday: _____	_____	
Saturday: _____	_____	
Sunday: _____		
Notes: _____		

Current Strengths: Current Self Rank: _____

Areas that you feel are working well for you. Can be max lifts, mechanics, mental strengths, etc.

Things to work on:

Areas you feel need to be improved upon in order to reach your goals.

Weekly Reflections

Big Victories This Week   Areas You Improved

How I felt this week:
Outstanding | Excellent | Great | Good | Bad

Massive Purpose.   Relentless Intent.   Super Success.

Monthly Review

Super Successes:

These are targeted success you have had this month. Triumphs that will help you reach your goal.

_____
_____
_____

How Will These Super Successes Help You Reach Your One-year Goal?

_____
_____
_____
_____

Biggest Difficulties:

What were some difficulties this month that stood in your way of accomplishing more?

_____
_____
_____
_____   _____

How Can You Improve Next Month?

List any improvements you could have made looking back?

_____
_____
_____
_____

What Did You Learn From The Previous Month?

List major takeaways.

_____
_____
_____

Who Could Have Helped You Last Month?

List individuals that you know that could have helped you last month and see if you can ask them for advice heading into your new month.

_____
_____

I Had Relentless Intent This Month: Y/N
I Accomplished My Month with Massive Purpose: Y/N
I Was a Super Success This Month: Y / N

Success Notes

Control Your Day [S.M.A.R.T]
Specific | Measurable | Achievable | Relevant | Time Bound

Monday
Goals   Actions   Workouts   Food   Water   **Mood Meter**

Tuesday
Goals   Actions   Workouts   Food   Water   **Mood Meter**

Wednesday
Goals   Actions   Workouts   Food   Water   **Mood Meter**

Thursday
Goals   Actions   Workouts   Food   Water   **Mood Meter**

Friday
Goals   Actions   Workouts   Food   Water   **Mood Meter**

Saturday
Goals   Actions   Workouts   Food   Water   **Mood Meter**

Sunday
Goals   Actions   Workouts   Food   Water   **Mood Meter**

Control Your Week of Success

"What makes something special is not just what you have to gain, but what you feel there is to lose." - Andre Agassi

Date:	Weekly Goals	Week#

_____
_____
_____
_____

Training Days	Weekly Drills	Power C's To Reflect On
Monday: _____	_____	**Used to help you retain focus to achieve your goals**
Tuesday: _____	_____	
Wednesday: _____	_____	
Thursday: _____	_____	_____
Friday: _____	_____	_____
Saturday: _____	_____	_____
Sunday: _____		_____
Notes: _____		_____
_____		_____
_____		

Current Strengths: Current Self Rank: _____

Areas that you feel are working well for you. Can be max lifts, mechanics, mental strengths, etc.

_____
_____
_____

Things to work on:

Areas you feel need to be improved upon in order to reach your goals.

_____
_____
_____

Weekly Reflections

Big Victories This Week   Areas You Improved
_____   _____
_____   _____
_____   _____

How I felt this week:
Outstanding | Excellent | Great | Good | Bad

Massive Purpose.   Relentless Intent.   Super Success.

Control Your Week of Success

"A trophy carries dust. Memories last forever." - Mary Lou Retton

Date:	Weekly Goals	Week#

_____
_____
_____
_____

Training Days	Weekly Drills	Power C's To Reflect On
Monday: _____	_____	**Used to help you retain focus to achieve your goals**
Tuesday: _____	_____	
Wednesday: _____	_____	_____
Thursday: _____	_____	_____
Friday: _____	_____	_____
Saturday: _____	_____	_____
Sunday: _____		_____
Notes: _____		_____
_____		_____
_____		

Current Strengths: Current Self Rank: _____

Areas that you feel are working well for you. Can be max lifts, mechanics, mental strengths, etc.

_____
_____
_____

Things to work on:

Areas you feel need to be improved upon in order to reach your goals.

_____
_____
_____

Weekly Reflections

Big Victories This Week   Areas You Improved
_____   _____
_____   _____
_____   _____

How I felt this week:
Outstanding | Excellent | Great | Good | Bad

Control Your Week of Success

"Nobody beat Vitas Gerulaitis 17 times in a row." - Vitas Gerulaitis

Date:	Weekly Goals	Week#

_____

_____

_____

_____

Training Days	Weekly Drills	Power C's To Reflect On
Monday: _____	_____	**Used to help you retain focus to achieve your goals**
Tuesday: _____	_____	
Wednesday: _____	_____	_____
Thursday: _____	_____	_____
Friday: _____	_____	_____
Saturday: _____	_____	_____
Sunday: _____		_____
Notes: _____		_____
_____		
_____		

Current Strengths: Current Self Rank: _____

Areas that you feel are working well for you. Can be max lifts, mechanics, mental strengths, etc.

_____

_____

_____

Things to work on:

Areas you feel need to be improved upon in order to reach your goals.

_____

_____

_____

Weekly Reflections

Big Victories This Week   Areas You Improved

_____   _____

_____   _____

_____   _____

How I felt this week:
Outstanding | Excellent | Great | Good | Bad

Control Your Week of Success

"I never worry about the problem. I worry about the solution." - Shaquille O'Neal

Date:	Weekly Goals	Week#

_____

_____

_____

_____

Training Days	Weekly Drills	Power C's To Reflect On
Monday: _____	_____	**Used to help you retain focus to achieve your goals**
Tuesday: _____	_____	
Wednesday: _____	_____	_____
Thursday: _____	_____	_____
Friday: _____	_____	_____
Saturday: _____	_____	_____
Sunday: _____		_____
Notes: _____		_____
_____		_____
_____		

Current Strengths: Current Self Rank: _____

Areas that you feel are working well for you. Can be max lifts, mechanics, mental strengths, etc.

_____

_____

_____

Things to work on:

Areas you feel need to be improved upon in order to reach your goals.

_____

_____

_____

Weekly Reflections

Big Victories This Week   Areas You Improved

_____   _____

_____   _____

_____   _____

How I felt this week:
Outstanding | Excellent | Great | Good | Bad

Monthly Review

Super Successes:

These are targeted success you have had this month. Triumphs that will help you reach your goal.

_____
_____
_____

How Will These Super Successes Help You Reach Your One-year Goal?

_____
_____
_____
_____

Biggest Difficulties:

What were some difficulties this month that stood in your way of accomplishing more?

_____
_____
_____
_____   _____

How Can You Improve Next Month?

List any improvements you could have made looking back?

_____
_____
_____
_____

What Did You Learn From The Previous Month?

List major takeaways.

_____
_____
_____

Who Could Have Helped You Last Month?

List individuals that you know that could have helped you last month and see if you can ask them for advice heading into your new month.

_____
_____

I Had Relentless Intent This Month: Y/N
I Accomplished My Month with Massive Purpose: Y/N
I Was a Super Success This Month: Y / N

Success Notes

Control Your Day [S.M.A.R.T]

Specific | Measurable | Achievable | Relevant | Time Bound

Monday

Goals	Actions	Workouts	Food	Water	Mood Meter

Tuesday

Goals	Actions	Workouts	Food	Water	Mood Meter

Wednesday

Goals	Actions	Workouts	Food	Water	Mood Meter

Thursday

Goals	Actions	Workouts	Food	Water	Mood Meter

Friday

Goals	Actions	Workouts	Food	Water	Mood Meter

Saturday

Goals	Actions	Workouts	Food	Water	Mood Meter

Sunday

Goals	Actions	Workouts	Food	Water	Mood Meter

Control Your Week of Success

"If you are afraid of failure you don't deserve to be successful!" - Charles Barkley

Date:	Weekly Goals	Week#

_____

Training Days	Weekly Drills	Power C's To Reflect On
Monday: _____	_____	**Used to help you retain focus to achieve your goals**
Tuesday: _____	_____	
Wednesday: _____	_____	_____
Thursday: _____	_____	_____
Friday: _____	_____	_____
Saturday: _____	_____	_____
Sunday: _____		_____
Notes: _____		_____
_____		_____
_____		

Current Strengths: Current Self Rank: _____

Areas that you feel are working well for you. Can be max lifts, mechanics, mental strengths, etc.

_____
_____
_____

Things to work on:

Areas you feel need to be improved upon in order to reach your goals.

_____
_____
_____

Weekly Reflections

Big Victories This Week   Areas You Improved

_____   _____

_____   _____

_____   _____

How I felt this week:
Outstanding | Excellent | Great | Good | Bad

Control Your Week of Success

"I've learned that something constructive comes from every defeat." - Tom Landry

Date:	Weekly Goals	Week#

_____

_____

_____

_____

Training Days	Weekly Drills	Power C's To Reflect On
Monday: _____	_____	**Used to help you retain focus to achieve your goals**
Tuesday: _____	_____	
Wednesday: _____	_____	_____
Thursday: _____	_____	_____
Friday: _____	_____	_____
Saturday: _____	_____	_____
Sunday: _____		_____
Notes: _____		_____
_____		_____
_____		

Current Strengths: Current Self Rank: _____

Areas that you feel are working well for you. Can be max lifts, mechanics, mental strengths, etc.

_____

_____

_____

Things to work on:

Areas you feel need to be improved upon in order to reach your goals.

_____

_____

_____

Weekly Reflections

Big Victories This Week   Areas You Improved

_____   _____

_____   _____

_____   _____

How I felt this week:
Outstanding | Excellent | Great | Good | Bad

Control Your Week of Success

"You're never a loser until you quit trying." - Mike Ditka

Date:	Weekly Goals	Week#

_____
_____
_____
_____

Training Days	Weekly Drills	Power C's To Reflect On
Monday: _____	_____	**Used to help you retain focus to achieve your goals**
Tuesday: _____	_____	
Wednesday: _____	_____	_____
Thursday: _____	_____	_____
Friday: _____	_____	_____
Saturday: _____	_____	_____
Sunday: _____		_____
Notes: _____		_____
_____		
_____		

Current Strengths:　　　　　　　　　　　Current Self Rank: _____

Areas that you feel are working well for you. Can be max lifts, mechanics, mental strengths, etc.

_____
_____
_____

Things to work on:

Areas you feel need to be improved upon in order to reach your goals.

_____
_____
_____

Weekly Reflections

Big Victories This Week　　　　　　　　Areas You Improved

_____　　　　　　　_____
_____　　　　　　　_____
_____　　　　　　　_____

How I felt this week:
Outstanding | Excellent | Great | Good | Bad

Control Your Week of Success

"If a team wants to intimidate you physically and you let them, they've won." - Mia Hamm

Date:	Weekly Goals	Week#

_____

_____

_____

_____

Training Days	Weekly Drills	Power C's To Reflect On
Monday: _____	_____	**Used to help you retain focus to achieve your goals**
Tuesday: _____	_____	
Wednesday: _____	_____	_____
Thursday: _____	_____	_____
Friday: _____	_____	_____
Saturday: _____		_____
Sunday: _____		_____
Notes: _____		_____
_____		
_____		

Current Strengths: Current Self Rank: _____

Areas that you feel are working well for you. Can be max lifts, mechanics, mental strengths, etc.

_____

_____

_____

Things to work on:

Areas you feel need to be improved upon in order to reach your goals.

_____

_____

_____

Weekly Reflections

Big Victories This Week   Areas You Improved

_____   _____

_____   _____

_____   _____

How I felt this week:
Outstanding | Excellent | Great | Good | Bad

Monthly Review

Super Successes:

These are targeted success you have had this month. Triumphs that will help you reach your goal.

_____
_____
_____

How Will These Super Successes Help You Reach Your One-year Goal?

_____
_____
_____
_____

Biggest Difficulties:

What were some difficulties this month that stood in your way of accomplishing more?

_____
_____
_____
_____   _____

How Can You Improve Next Month?

List any improvements you could have made looking back?

_____
_____
_____
_____

What Did You Learn From The Previous Month?

List major takeaways.

_____
_____
_____

Who Could Have Helped You Last Month?

List individuals that you know that could have helped you last month and see if you can ask them for advice heading into your new month.

_____
_____

I Had Relentless Intent This Month: Y/N
I Accomplished My Month with Massive Purpose: Y/N
I Was a Super Success This Month: Y / N

Success Notes

Control Your Day [S.M.A.R.T]

Specific | **M**easurable | **A**chievable | **R**elevant | **T**ime Bound

Monday

Goals	Actions	Workouts	Food	Water

Mood Meter

Tuesday

Goals	Actions	Workouts	Food	Water

Mood Meter

Wednesday

Goals	Actions	Workouts	Food	Water

Mood Meter

Thursday

Goals	Actions	Workouts	Food	Water

Mood Meter

Friday

Goals	Actions	Workouts	Food	Water

Mood Meter

Saturday

Goals	Actions	Workouts	Food	Water

Mood Meter

Sunday

Goals	Actions	Workouts	Food	Water

Mood Meter

Control Your Week of Success

"He who is not courageous enough to take risks will accomplish nothing in life." -
Muhammad Ali

Date:	Weekly Goals	Week#

_____

_____

_____

_____

Training Days	Weekly Drills	Power C's To Reflect On
Monday: _____	_____	**Used to help you retain focus to achieve your goals**
Tuesday: _____	_____	
Wednesday: _____	_____	_____
Thursday: _____	_____	_____
Friday: _____	_____	_____
Saturday: _____		_____
Sunday: _____		_____
Notes: _____		_____
_____		_____
_____		

Current Strengths: Current Self Rank: _____

Areas that you feel are working well for you. Can be max lifts, mechanics, mental strengths, etc.

_____

_____

_____

Things to work on:

Areas you feel need to be improved upon in order to reach your goals.

_____

_____

_____

Weekly Reflections

Big Victories This Week   Areas You Improved

_____   _____

_____   _____

_____   _____

How I felt this week:
Outstanding | Excellent | Great | Good | Bad

Massive Purpose.   Relentless Intent.   Super Success.

Control Your Week of Success

"It is not the size of a man but the size of his heart that matters." - Evander Holyfield

Date:	Weekly Goals	Week#

_____
_____
_____
_____

Training Days	Weekly Drills	Power C's To Reflect On
Monday: _____	_____	**Used to help you retain focus to achieve your goals**
Tuesday: _____	_____	
Wednesday: _____	_____	_____
Thursday: _____	_____	_____
Friday: _____	_____	_____
Saturday: _____	_____	_____
Sunday: _____		_____
Notes: _____		_____
_____		_____
_____		

Current Strengths: Current Self Rank: _____

Areas that you feel are working well for you. Can be max lifts, mechanics, mental strengths, etc.

_____
_____
_____

Things to work on:

Areas you feel need to be improved upon in order to reach your goals.

_____
_____
_____

Weekly Reflections

Big Victories This Week   Areas You Improved

_____   _____
_____   _____
_____   _____

How I felt this week:
Outstanding | Excellent | Great | Good | Bad

Control Your Week of Success

"Persistence can change failure into extraordinary achievement." - Matt Biondi

Date:	Weekly Goals	Week#

_____
_____
_____
_____

Training Days	Weekly Drills	Power C's To Reflect On
Monday: _____	_____	**Used to help you retain focus to achieve your goals**
Tuesday: _____	_____	
Wednesday: _____	_____	
Thursday: _____	_____	_____
Friday: _____	_____	_____
Saturday: _____	_____	_____
Sunday: _____		_____
Notes: _____		_____
_____		_____
_____		

Current Strengths: **Current Self Rank: _____**

Areas that you feel are working well for you. Can be max lifts, mechanics, mental strengths, etc.

_____
_____
_____

Things to work on:

Areas you feel need to be improved upon in order to reach your goals.

_____
_____
_____

Weekly Reflections

Big Victories This Week   **Areas You Improved**

_____   _____
_____   _____
_____   _____

How I felt this week:
Outstanding | Excellent | Great | Good | Bad

Massive Purpose.   Relentless Intent.   Super Success.
Control Your Week of Success

"To give any less than your best is to sacrifice a gift." - Steve Prefontaine

Date:	Weekly Goals	Week#

_____

Training Days
Monday: _____
Tuesday: _____
Wednesday: _____
Thursday: _____
Friday: _____
Saturday: _____
Sunday: _____
Notes: _____
_____
_____

Weekly Drills
_____
_____
_____
_____
_____
_____

Power C's To Reflect On
Used to help you retain focus to achieve your goals
_____
_____
_____
_____
_____

Current Strengths: Current Self Rank: _____

Areas that you feel are working well for you. Can be max lifts, mechanics, mental strengths, etc.
_____
_____
_____

Things to work on:

Areas you feel need to be improved upon in order to reach your goals.
_____
_____
_____

Weekly Reflections

Big Victories This Week   Areas You Improved
_____   _____
_____   _____
_____   _____

How I felt this week:
Outstanding | Excellent | Great | Good | Bad

Monthly Review

Super Successes:

These are targeted success you have had this month. Triumphs that will help you reach your goal.

_____

_____

_____

How Will These Super Successes Help You Reach Your One-year Goal?

_____

_____

_____

_____

Biggest Difficulties:

What were some difficulties this month that stood in your way of accomplishing more?

_____

_____

_____

_____   _____

How Can You Improve Next Month?

List any improvements you could have made looking back?

_____

_____

_____

_____   _____

What Did You Learn From The Previous Month?

List major takeaways.

_____

_____

_____

Who Could Have Helped You Last Month?

List individuals that you know that could have helped you last month and see if you can ask them for advice heading into your new month.

_____

_____

I Had Relentless Intent This Month: Y/N
I Accomplished My Month with Massive Purpose: Y/N
I Was a Super Success This Month: Y / N

Massive Purpose.   Relentless Intent.   Super Success.

Success Notes

Control Your Day [S.M.A.R.T]

Specific | Measurable | Achievable | Relevant | Time Bound

Monday
Goals	Actions	Workouts	Food	Water	Mood Meter

Tuesday
Goals	Actions	Workouts	Food	Water	Mood Meter

Wednesday
Goals	Actions	Workouts	Food	Water	Mood Meter

Thursday
Goals	Actions	Workouts	Food	Water	Mood Meter

Friday
Goals	Actions	Workouts	Food	Water	Mood Meter

Saturday
Goals	Actions	Workouts	Food	Water	Mood Meter

Sunday
Goals	Actions	Workouts	Food	Water	Mood Meter

Control Your Week of Success

"If you believe it, the mind can achieve it." -Ronnie Lott

Date:	Weekly Goals	Week#

_____

_____

_____

_____

Training Days	Weekly Drills	Power C's To Reflect On
Monday: _____	_____	**Used to help you retain focus to achieve your goals**
Tuesday: _____	_____	
Wednesday: _____	_____	_____
Thursday: _____	_____	_____
Friday: _____	_____	_____
Saturday: _____	_____	_____
Sunday: _____		_____
Notes: _____		_____
_____		_____
_____		

Current Strengths: Current Self Rank: _____

Areas that you feel are working well for you. Can be max lifts, mechanics, mental strengths, etc.

_____

_____

_____

Things to work on:

Areas you feel need to be improved upon in order to reach your goals.

_____

_____

_____

Weekly Reflections

Big Victories This Week   Areas You Improved

_____   _____

_____   _____

_____   _____

How I felt this week:
Outstanding | Excellent | Great | Good | Bad

Control Your Week of Success

"If you train hard, you'll not only be hard, you'll be hard to beat." - Herschel Walker

Date:	Weekly Goals	Week#

_____

_____

_____

_____

Training Days	Weekly Drills	Power C's To Reflect On
Monday: _____	_____	**Used to help you retain focus to achieve your goals**
Tuesday: _____	_____	
Wednesday: _____	_____	_____
Thursday: _____	_____	_____
Friday: _____	_____	_____
Saturday: _____	_____	_____
Sunday: _____		_____
Notes: _____		_____
_____		
_____		

Current Strengths: Current Self Rank: _____

Areas that you feel are working well for you. Can be max lifts, mechanics, mental strengths, etc.

_____

_____

_____

Things to work on:

Areas you feel need to be improved upon in order to reach your goals.

_____

_____

_____

Weekly Reflections

Big Victories This Week   Areas You Improved

_____   _____

_____   _____

_____   _____

How I felt this week:
Outstanding | Excellent | Great | Good | Bad

Control Your Week of Success

"Never say never because limits, like fears, are often just illusion." -Michael Jordan

Date:	Weekly Goals	Week#

_____
_____
_____
_____

Training Days	Weekly Drills	Power C's To Reflect On
Monday: _____	_____	**Used to help you retain focus to achieve your goals**
Tuesday: _____	_____	
Wednesday: _____	_____	_____
Thursday: _____	_____	_____
Friday: _____	_____	_____
Saturday: _____	_____	_____
Sunday: _____		_____
Notes: _____		_____
_____		_____
_____		

Current Strengths: Current Self Rank: _____

Areas that you feel are working well for you. Can be max lifts, mechanics, mental strengths, etc.

_____
_____
_____

Things to work on:

Areas you feel need to be improved upon in order to reach your goals.

_____
_____
_____

Weekly Reflections

Big Victories This Week   Areas You Improved

_____   _____
_____   _____
_____   _____

How I felt this week:
Outstanding | Excellent | Great | Good | Bad

Control Your Week of Success

"All I know is grind." -Ray Lewis

Date:	Weekly Goals	Week#

_____
_____
_____
_____

Training Days	Weekly Drills	Power C's To Reflect On
Monday: _____	_____	**Used to help you retain focus to achieve your goals**
Tuesday: _____	_____	
Wednesday: _____	_____	_____
Thursday: _____	_____	_____
Friday: _____	_____	_____
Saturday: _____	_____	_____
Sunday: _____		_____
Notes: _____		_____
_____		_____
_____		

Current Strengths: Current Self Rank: _____

Areas that you feel are working well for you. Can be max lifts, mechanics, mental strengths, etc.

_____
_____
_____

Things to work on:

Areas you feel need to be improved upon in order to reach your goals.

_____
_____
_____

Weekly Reflections

Big Victories This Week   Areas You Improved

_____   _____
_____   _____
_____   _____

How I felt this week:
Outstanding | Excellent | Great | Good | Bad

Monthly Review

Super Successes:

These are targeted success you have had this month. Triumphs that will help you reach your goal.

_____
_____
_____

How Will These Super Successes Help You Reach Your One-year Goal?

_____
_____
_____
_____

Biggest Difficulties:

What were some difficulties this month that stood in your way of accomplishing more?

_____
_____
_____
_____   _____

How Can You Improve Next Month?

List any improvements you could have made looking back?

_____
_____
_____
_____

What Did You Learn From The Previous Month?

List major takeaways.

_____
_____
_____

Who Could Have Helped You Last Month?

List individuals that you know that could have helped you last month and see if you can ask them for advice heading into your new month.

_____
_____

I Had Relentless Intent This Month: Y/N
I Accomplished My Month with Massive Purpose: Y/N
I Was a Super Success This Month: Y / N

Success Notes

Massive Purpose.   Relentless Intent.   Super Success.